THE
WALMART
CASHIER

Ronn Medow

PAGE PUBLISHING, INC.
New York, NY

First originally published by Page Publishing, Inc. 2014

ISBN 978-1-63417-488-6 (pbk)
ISBN 978-1-63417-489-3 (digital)

Printed in the United States of America

For my little bride.

"My name is Ozymandias, king of kings:
Look on my works, Ye Mighty, and despair."
— Shelley

"I don't get no respect."
—Jacob Rodney Cohen

CHAPTER 1

Becoming a Walmart Cashier

Working at Walmart is a post-retirement job for me. After retiring from Lexus of Reno at the end of August 2008, I worked at several different and interesting (interesting to me, but probably not to you) jobs, mostly part-time, including a few months working for the U.S. Census Bureau in 2010. In April 2011, I talked to a friendly acquaintance who was a co-manager at a Walmart store in Reno. Jake (not his real name) was also a customer of mine when I sold cars at Lexus of Reno.

By the way, I have changed the names of all the Walmart associates and customers to protect their privacy and anonymity, except my own name. I wanted to change my name, as well, to protect my own privacy and anonymity; but it quickly got complicated, and I just couldn't figure out how to make it work.

I had contacted Jake because I had access to some products that I was hoping to sell in the Reno Walmart stores. I went to Jake's store, maybe my third time ever in a Walmart, to pick up the forms required by Walmart. I learned that Jake's store was hiring, and the paperwork listing the procedures and requirements for placing and selling product was daunting.

Easily daunted, I recycled the paperwork and applied for a part-time job as a cashier. Personnel called me within two days to ask me to interview. The assistant manager who supervised the interview asked me who provided my paycheck. I told her the customer provided my paycheck. She was pleased, and I was hired as a part-time Walmart associate, a Walmart cashier. I would start at $9.25 an hour.

I was half pleased and half dismayed. Working would get me out of the house, but please keep in mind that it was April, the beginning of baseball season. And I spend (waste) hundreds of hours a year watching and listening to baseball games, especially San Francisco Giant games. And I like to think I know a few things about baseball. So getting out of the house meant I would miss a lot of baseball—live baseball. Fortunately, televised games can be recorded and enjoyed at one's convenience, so Theo, my little bride, and I record most of the games. She likes baseball too.

When I work 'til midnight, I often come home and watch the recorded game until the wee hours. Fast-forwarding through the commercials helps to shorten the length of time I spend in front of the screen, but I know this book would have been finished months ago if I didn't spend so much time watching baseball.

Also, working would help pay a few bills. Realistically, $9.25 an hour would not buy any big ticket items, and it has been many years since I worked for so little money. But $9.25 could pay a number of little bills and working part-time after working fifty-five to sixty-five hours a week in the car business seemed like a piece of cake.

In my experience, Walmart associates rarely talk about their pay in specific terms. The first time any associate said anything to me about pay was in September 2013, almost two and a half years after I started working at Walmart. A fairly new cashier mentioned that she was paid $8.65 an hour. Apparently, not everyone starts at the same rate of pay.

Well, enough of this drivel. I started working, and soon I was coming home with stories about the mostly funny things that happened at work. Theo is my best audience. She laughed at most of my "Walmart Stories" and sometimes she rated them.

Let me assure you that Theo is a woman, not a horse, and her rating system was based on her reaction to a given story. She doesn't just laugh. She might also snort and stomp. One snort and one stomp is a good story. Two snorts and three stomps is a really funny story.

As I tell you these stories, I don't expect you to snort and stomp (you could give it a try), but I do hope you will smile and laugh at the funny ones and feel appropriately sad when a story calls for a sad response. Three of the chapters are comprised of "Walmart Stories." If you don't like them, I'm in trouble.

CHAPTER 2

Walmart Stories I: On the Sales Floor

These are true stories, and they all took place on the sales floor or at my assigned register.

1. One day, I left my register to return a stray shopping cart to the place where the carts are supposed to hang out. A lady stopped me and asked, "Excuse me. Do you work here?"

"Allegedly, yes. How may I help you?" The lady seemed to be in her forties, and she was dressed very nicely.

She said, "I accidently dropped my keys in the trash barrel, and I don't want to reach down in that mess."

"So you want me to reach down in that mess?" I smiled to let her know I was teasing her. "I'll be happy to find your keys for you."

I leaned over into the big barrel and looked up at her. "Do you know about where you dropped them? Which side?" She leaned into the barrel to point out the approximate drop spot. Our faces were uncomfortably close.

I whispered to her, "We can't go on meeting like this," and I retrieved the keys.

She completed her shopping and checked out at someone else's register, then stopped at my register to thank me again.

2. On another occasion, I was returning a cart to the cart corral and a customer asked, "Can I use that cart?"

"Yes," I said. "But it has a noisy wheel."

He said, "OK then, I'll get a different one."

I continued talking. "About half of our carts have bad wheels, and we won't be satisfied until we're at 100 percent. I think we'll be successful."

I say many things I probably shouldn't say. I like to see the customers smile or laugh, and they usually do. But not always.

3. Two young women were busy talking as I rang up their purchase. They were discussing chocolate coconut milk. One asked, "Where do you get chocolate coconut milk, anyway?" She meant, "Where can you buy it?"

Ignoring her meaning, I said, "Chocolate coconuts."

She shot me a dirty look. Her friend laughed and said, "I get it. That was pretty good."

4. One night I was scheduled to work until midnight. About 11:30, a customer put several packages of beef jerky and a toilet plunger on the belt.

I couldn't resist commenting. "Sir, I'm not a doctor, but you might consider cutting back a little on the beef jerky."

5. The card reader at my register was having a bad day. Customers were swiping their debit cards and credit cards, and 46 percent of the time the reader wasn't picking up the info. I apologized to a lady customer and explained the problem as I swiped her card on my side of the register.

She said, "You must have old equipment."

I chose not to take her comment personally.

6. One evening, two women who seemed to be in a really good mood and/or tipsy approached my register. Each one was buying just a few items. The first woman reached into her sweater and took out two oranges. She put them on the counter in front of me. The women were laughing, almost out of control. I was smiling, a bit embarrassed, but willing to go along with the scenario. This kind of thing doesn't happen every day. I started to reach for the oranges then pulled my hands back. I asked, "May I touch them?" Lots more laughter.

7. Three little children were standing in front of my register as their parents were putting their groceries on the belt. As I was scanning and bagging, I guessed their ages, and my guesses were pretty accurate. The sister was ten and the little brothers were seven and five. Then I said, "Okay, now you have to guess how old I am."

With a huge smile on his face, the five-year-old said, "You are really old!"

I also like to tell the three- and four-year-olds, "You are very cute." If they smile, and they usually do, I ask, "Have you always been cute?"

Ninety percent of the time, they nod or say yes.

8. Returning to the sales floor after a break, I was approached by a woman who saw my name tag.

"Sir, can you tell me where the nuts are?"

"Ma'am," I said, "this is Walmart. The nuts are everywhere."

9. We have motorized shopping carts for customers who are unable to walk around the store. One night, a customer called my attention to a cart that had "urine all over it." I should have put a note on it. Instead, I went to find a customer service manager who could call a maintenance associate to clean up the cart. When I turned my attention back to the cart, I saw that another customer was already driving it. I was tempted to say, "Ma'am, urine the wrong cart." Frustrated, I muttered to myself, "P— on it."

10. One of our regular customers is a grouchy old man. He moves slowly, his hands shake, he has trouble hearing, and he never smiles. No wonder he's grouchy. I did not enjoy cashiering for him. One day he approached my register with several plastic containers of cookies. His hands were shaking, and he appeared to almost throw a container of cookies on the floor. Cookies flew in every direction. Now I don't dread waiting on him. When I see him, I smile to myself and think, "There's the man who tossed his cookies."

CHAPTER 3

Trivia Questions

Cashiering can be really boring work, so I have learned some ways to engage the customer and help pass the time.

One of these ways is to post trivia questions. I take a slip of register tape, print a trivia question, and tape it to the counter, facing the customers. Said customers may or may not see the question. They may or may not respond to the question. I don't prompt them or call their attention to the question.

A frequent response is "What do you win if you know the answer?" or words to that effect. I usually say something like, "Your prize is the satisfaction of knowing the answer when most customers did not." Or, "It's just for fun. It's Walmart, not Jeopardy." What I would like to say is "I wanted the prize to be a brand-new Lexus, but the billionaires in Arkansas said 'NO.'" A response like that might be considered sarcastic, and I work hard at avoiding sarcasm.

Others will ask, "Do you know the answer?" What I would like to say is, "Not until I get the text message from the Walton family in Arkansas. They send me the questions and the answers." Instead, I gently inform them that I make up the questions, so yes, I know the answers.

12

Multiple choice questions and true or false questions generate a much higher rate of response than questions that call for a specific answer. The responder has a better chance at answering correctly.

Rarely does a Walmart associate try to answer a trivia question. I think most customers, including Walmart associates, either do not notice the question or choose not to respond because they don't know the answer or they just don't care.

On the other hand, some of "my" customers seem to like the questions and look forward to participating. I have even had customers who brought trivia questions, verbally or typewritten, to me.

Here are a few of the questions, the answers, some of the responses, and a few more facts and observations.

If my rambling on irritates you, I apologize. Sometimes it irritates me too.

1. In what year did Nevada become a state?

Nevada became the thirty-sixth state on October 31, 1864. Officially, October 31 is Nevada Day, but since the year 2000, Nevada Day has been observed on the last Friday in October. October 31 is also Halloween, but you already knew that. If you study the history of Halloween, you will learn how souling, mumming, and guising eventually led to our trick or treat custom. There was no trick or treat in Nevada in 1864. My customers' guesses about statehood ranged from 1720 to 1918. Now let us think about this. What was going on in 1720? MDCCXX (I like Roman numerals) was a leap year. Benjamin Franklin was fourteen years old. The population of the American colonies was about 475,000. The largest cities were Boston, Philadelphia, and New York with populations of approximately twelve thousand, ten thousand, and seven thousand respectively.

After 1720, a number of other events, some of them interesting but too numerous to mention here, took place in the United States and in Nevada; and before you knew it, the year was 1864. Time flies when you're having fun. Well, that's hardly fair. You might find a few facts about Nevada's becoming a state interesting.

2. How did Reno, Nevada, get its name? This was a multiple choice question, and here are the choices.

A. The Reno Kid

B. Jesse Reno

C. James Reno Donner

D. Named after settlers from Reno, Texas

The correct answer is B, Jesse Reno. He was Major General Jesse Lee Reno of the Union Army. He died in battle on September 14, 1862, near Boonsboro, Maryland. The town of Reno was officially designated on May 9, 1868. El Reno, Oklahoma, Reno, Pennsylvania, and Reno County, Kansas, were also named in his honor.

There are two towns in Texas named Reno, one near Fort Worth, and one near Paris. (I heard it through the grapevine.) The two Renos (or is it Renoes?) are about five inches apart on my Relais and Chateaux North American Road Atlas. You could do the math, but being in a fairly magnanimous mood at this instant, I will do the math for you. Okay, that's roughly 150 miles apart.

Imagine a traveler driving in Texas and asking for help. "Which way is Reno?"

The Texan answering the question could point in two different directions and ask, "Which one?"

I spent a great deal of time trying to determine whether either Reno, Texas, was named after Jesse Reno. After ten minutes, I gave up and decided it would have to be one of those unsolved mysteries that fill my life.

By the way, one of Jesse Lee Reno's five children, Jesse W. Reno, produced and installed the first working escalator in 1896.

A number of people guessed C, James Reno Donner, but I made up that name. A bit of misdirection. I figured the Donner name would encourage a few wrong answers. If you live in Nevada, you know something about the Donner Party. The Donner Party refers to a group of families and individuals who, in 1846, were trying to use a shortcut to get to California. Behind schedule, they were trapped in a snowstorm in the Sierra Nevada mountains. Forty-five of the eighty-one died, and many of the survivors allegedly resorted to cannibalism in order to save their own lives. Some party, huh? The complete story is really fascinating, and I'm sure some folks, upon hearing or reading about the Donner Party, ask themselves, "What would I have done?" It's easy to sit on your couch, surrounded by candy and chips and pizza and soft drinks and beer, and say, "Oh, I could never do that. I would starve to death before I could eat human flesh." But when you're freezing and starving and delirious all at the same time, you might choose to live. Just a little food for thought.

Ohhhh, sorry about that.

3. What is Lithia?
   A. An element
   B. Lithium oxide
   C. A country is Eastern Europe
   D. A group of car and truck dealerships

Some people guessed A or C, but the correct answers are both B and D. I hardly expect anyone to know what lithium oxide is, but the Lithia organization, which is listed on the New York Stock Exchange (LAD), currently has four dealerships in Reno and over 110 dealerships in United States, mostly in the west and southwest.

By the way, when Theo and I visited Reno in October 2002, to determine whether or not we wanted to live here, I went to the personnel office in one of the Lithia stores to apply for a sales position. They were not impressed with me or my credentials—no job offer. After I had sold at Lexus of Reno for about two years, Lithia started calling me and two or three other Lexus salespeople to try to recruit us into their organization.

Not one of us was interested. Our sales manager was difficult—I thought he was half genius and half idiot—but we were all selling cars and making a living. Some made six figures. And the Lexus vehicles were and are incredibly wonderful.

Lithia is also the name of an unincorporated community in Florida, and that was not part of the trivia question. That brings us back to lithium oxide. If you absolutely have to know more about lithia, or lithium oxide, please check out Wikipedia. My skills as a chemist are very basic and quite consistent. Everything I touch turns into something else.

4. Who is Carson City named for?
   A. Carson Pirie Scott
   B. Christopher Houston Carson
   C. Rachel Carson
   D. Johnny Carson

The correct answer is B. I was amused by the fact that a number of folks chose answer A. Carson Pirie Scott, now shortened to Carson's, is a chain of department stores founded by Samuel Carson in 1854, but there are no such stores in Nevada or California.

Nobody guessed Johnny Carson, and sadly, nobody knew the name Rachel Carson.

Christopher Houston Carson is better known as Kit Carson. If I had offered Kit Carson as an answer, the question would have been way too easy.

Kit Carson and Abraham Lincoln were both born in 1809 in Kentucky. Their birthplaces are about one hundred miles apart. (By the way, Charles Darwin and Abraham Lincoln were born the same day; however, Darwin was not born in Kentucky. Mitch McConnell and Rand Paul are probably happy about that.)

5. Where was Kit Carson buried?
   A. Arlington National Cemetery
   B. Westminster Abbey
   C. Taos, New Mexico
   D. Carson City, Nevada

The correct answer is C. Taos was the home of Carson's third wife, Josefa Jaramillo, with whom he fathered eight children. Taos is also the home of the Kit Carson Home and Museum. Josefa died from childbirth complications on April 23, 1868, and Kit Carson died a month later. Two customers said Arlington, several said Carson City, and one guessed Westminster Abbey.

Charles Darwin is interred in Westminster Abbey.

6. Groucho, Chico, Harpo, Gummo, and Zeppo were the nicknames of the famous Marx brothers. Which name below was not the real name of any of the Marx brothers?
    A. Arthur
    B. Herbert
    C. Julius
    D. Karl
    E. Leonard
    F. Milton

Several people who guessed wrong seemed almost embarrassed when I told them the correct answer. Here are the matchups.

    A. Arthur is Harpo
    B. Herbert is Zeppo
    C. Julius is Groucho
    D. Karl
    E. Leonard is Chico
    F. Milton is Gummo

So there you have it, indisputable proof that Karl Marx was not one of the Marx brothers. Brought to you by your Walmart cashier. Karl Marx died in 1883 before any of the Marx brothers was born. He was an economist and philosopher. He was a prolific writer. You may have heard of *The Communist Manifesto* and *Das Kapital*? If you are now inspired to read about Karl Marx, I suggest that you also look up Karl's good buddy, Friedrich Engels.

7. Washoe County borders how many counties? (Reno is in Washoe County.)

    A. 6

    B. 9

    C. 11

    D. 13

Thirteen counties border Washoe County—six in Nevada, five in California, and two in Oregon. Most participants thought only in terms of Nevada counties, so they guessed A. Sometimes you have to think beyond the borders, outside the box. (Foreshadowing chapter 15.)

Finally one woman said 13. "Correct!" I said. "How did you know?" I was almost excited that someone got the answer right.

She said, "Because today is Friday the thirteenth." A true daughter of Nevada.

8. The Nutcracker ballet is traditionally performed during Christmas season. Who wrote the music?

    A. Beethoven

    B. Mozart

    C. Billy Joel

    D. Tchaikovsky

Of the few who responded, most guessed Beethoven or Mozart. The correct answer is Tchaikovsky, the Russian composer who lived from 1840 to 1893.

In 1891, he visited the United States and conducted the inaugural concert at Carnegie Hall.

Tchaikovsky and Tolstoy met on several occasions in 1876 and talked, mostly about music and the arts. My impression is that the great composer was intimidated by the great author. I read that on more than one occasion, Tchaikovsky saw Tolstoy on the streets of Moscow and went out of his way to avoid having to talk to him.

The Nutcracker was completed and first performed in 1892. Tchaikovsky died of complications from cholera in 1893. There is speculation about the possibility that he deliberately drank tainted water in an attempt to kill himself.

The man whose works, *The Nutcracker*, *Swan Lake*, and *The Sleeping Beauty*, to name a few, have brought joy to many millions of people suffered a sad and terrible death.

Beethoven and Mozart, who happen to be my favorite classical composers, also led incredibly interesting lives. I could write many, many pages about their lives and their brilliance, but not in this book. Maybe in *The Walmart Cashier Strikes Again*.

I do want to say a word about Billy Joel. Including his name in the list of possible answers is my attempt at offering a bit of humor, but I mean no disrespect. Billy Joel was and is a great songwriter and entertainer. One of our very best.

Billy Joel is about 5'5". Kit Carson was also about 5'5". You can roll your eyes at me as you read this, but knowing facts like these could save your life; for example, you could be walking in a dead end alley and someone could put a gun in your face and demand an answer. "How tall is Billy Joel? How tall was Kit Carson?"

The Walmart Cashier needs some sleep. And he really needs a decent editor.

9. Which is the westernmost city?
   A. Spokane, Washington
   B. Reno, Nevada
   C. Los Angeles, California
   D. San Diego, California
   E. Fresno, California

This question is what I call a "barroom bet" question. The correct answer is Reno, and many folks say it doesn't seem right. Here are the longitudes of each city, rounded off to the fourth decimal place:

Spokane	117.4260 W
Reno	119.8138 W
Los Angeles	118.2437 W
San Diego	117.1573 W
Fresno	119.7726 W

More than you wanted to know? Sorry. I'm guilty once again.

10. These U.S. presidents also served as vice presidents. Which ones served longer as VP than as president?

A. Lyndon Baines Johnson

B. Richard M. Nixon

C. Gerald Ford

D. Millard Fillmore

E. George H. W. Bush

F. John Adams

Correct answers are Adams, Nixon, and Bush.

To some extent, this question can be answered by using logic if you ask yourself which ones served two full terms as VP. Adams served eight years as VP to Washington, Nixon served eight years as VP to Eisenhower, and Bush served eight years as VP to Reagan.

Adams and Bush were one-term presidents. Adams lost his bid for reelection to Jefferson and Bush lost to Bill Clinton, whose middle name is Jefferson.

In 1796, Adams won the presidency over Jefferson, 71 electoral votes to 68. In those days, the candidate who received the second highest number of votes was elected vice president. It did not take long for our leaders to change that procedure—in 1804 they made a change. Candidates for president and vice president were placed on separate ballots.

In his bid for reelection in 1800, Adams received 65 electoral votes, Jefferson 73. But wait—there's more. Aaron Burr also received 73. The House of Representatives had to decide the outcome with each state delegation casting one vote. Through the first thirty-five ballots, no winner was determined. On the thirty-sixth ballot, largely through the influence of Alexander Hamilton, Jefferson was elected president and Burr was elected vice president. Jefferson received 10 votes, Burr 4. Two states made no choice.

Hamilton and Burr had been friendly earlier in their careers, but as time and events passed, they became bitter enemies. In 1804, when Burr was still vice president, the two fought a duel, and Burr killed Hamilton.

Dear reader, politics back then were just as ugly and nasty as they are now. We simply have more and faster ways of communicating now than we did then.

Nixon's second term as president was not completed, and he resigned on August 9, 1974. The famous Watergate scandal was Nixon's undoing. Nixon's first VP was Spiro Agnew, who resigned from office October 10, 1973, after a negotiated settlement was reached for tax evasion; although it appears that he was guilty of much more, including receiving bribes and payoffs when he was governor of Maryland. Nixon nominated Gerald Ford to be VP, and Ford was confirmed by Congress. When Nixon resigned, Gerald Ford became president.

Think about this—Gerald Ford became VP and then president without being elected to either office! Gerald Ford nominated Nelson Rockefeller to be his VP, and Congress confirmed this nomination.

When he actually ran for the presidency, President Ford lost to Jimmy Carter, but Rockefeller was not on the ticket. Bob Dole was the Republican candidate for vice president in 1976.

LBJ was VP for a short period of time because of John F. Kennedy's assassination, but I should not talk about LBJ. I hold a grudge.

In spite of LBJ's domestic accomplishments, I can never forgive him for increasing the U.S. involvement in the Vietnam war and for not negotiating an end to the war when he could have.

It cost him the opportunity to run for another term in 1968, but far worse, it cost our country some twenty thousand additional American lives and tens of thousands of additional war injuries.

And Millard Fillmore? He was VP to Zachary Taylor, who died in 1850 after sixteen months in office. Taylor's death occurred amid bizarre circumstances, and his body was exhumed in 1991 for tests and analysis. He may have been assassinated by poisoning. Or not. There is no clear proof either way.

Overzealous doctors probably hastened his death, and this all happened when malpractice suits were starting to become widespread. FYI, the American Medical Association was founded in 1847.

Millard Fillmore is not considered to have been one of our better presidents, but before he was elected to national office, he co-founded the University at Buffalo. He also was deeply involved in establishing Buffalo General Hospital in 1855 and the Buffalo Historical Society in 1862.

11. Which presidents died on the Fourth of July?
    A. James Monroe
    B. Dwight D. Eisenhower
    C. John Adams
    D. Teddy Roosevelt
    E. Andrew Jackson
    F. Thomas Jefferson

Thomas Jefferson and John Adams both died on July 4, 1826, Jefferson a few hours before Adams.

James Monroe died on July 4, 1831. While they were active in politics and in office, Adams and Jefferson were intense rivals. They later carried on a vigorous correspondence that went on for years. And Abigail Adams, who was no slouch, also corresponded with Jefferson. These people were so brilliant! What the heck happened?

12. "My Old Kentucky Home" is the state song of Kentucky. Who composed it?
    A. Daniel Boone
    B. Mark Twain
    C. Mitch McConnell
    D. Davy Crockett
    E. Stephen Foster

Stephen Foster composed "My Old Kentucky Home" and over two hundred other songs, including "O Susanna," "Jeanie with the Light Brown Hair," "Camptown Races," and "Beautiful Dreamer." He was America's first great songwriter. Sadly, nobody knew it while he was alive.

Foster was born on July 4, 1826, the same day that Jefferson and Adams died.

Foster's life was difficult. He was an alcoholic. His wife and daughter left him in New York and moved back to Pittsburgh. Foster lived in a cheap hotel on the Bowery. He died with pennies in his pocket. He was thirty-seven years old.

Several customers guessed that the composer was Mitch McConnell, which I found incredibly amusing. At this moment, the two U.S. senators from Kentucky are Rand Paul and Mitch McConnell, which I find incredibly amusing.

"O Susanna" was published on February 25, 1848. Karl Marx and Friedrich Engels published *The Communist Manifesto* four days earlier on February 21, 1848. Coincidence?

CHAPTER 4

Celebrities

Sometimes as I go about my duties at Walmart, I pass the time thinking about celebrities, their birth names, and their stage or screen names.

You might enjoy this little quiz. Or you might not!

The answers are at the end of the quiz, along with some comments and observations that trend toward stream of consciousness. Into the brain and onto the page.

1. The 1959 film *Operation Petticoat* starred two actors whose birth names were Archibald Alexander Leach and Bernard Schwartz. By what names do we know them?

2. Jerome Silberman starred in a number of films including *The Producers*, *Blazing Saddles*, and *Young Frankenstein*. These three movies were directed by Melvin James Kaminsky, who was married to Anna Maria Louisa Italiano. What are their professional names?

3. VH1's Divas Live 1999 concert featured a rendition of "Proud Mary" with Anna Mae Bullock (who has been one of my favorite singers for over fifty years), Cherilyn Sarkisian, and Reginald Dwight. By what names do we know these superstars?

4. The movie *Ghost* starred Caryn Elaine Johnson, Demetria Gene Guynes, and Patrick Swayze. What are the screen names of the two ladies?

5. Virginia Katherine McMath and Frederick Austerlitz gave us some of the best dancing ever shown on film. Who are these famous people?

6. Nathan Birnbaum and Benjamin Kubelsky were show business pioneers, icons, and two of my favorite entertainers. They were also very close friends. By what names do we know them?

7. Henry John Deutschendorf Jr. was a wonderful singer, songwriter, and actor. He was also an activist. What is his celebrity name?

8. One of our favorite actors, Tom Hanks, starred in *Joe Versus the Volcano*, *Sleepless in Seattle*, and *You've Got Mail*, with one of our favorite actresses whose birth name is Margaret Mary Emily Anne Hyra. How is she known professionally?

9. February 3, 1959, was "The Day the Music Died." A plane crash in Iowa took the lives of Charles Hardin Holley, Richard Steven Valenzuela, and Jiles Perry Richardson, and the plane's pilot, Roger Peterson. Who were these young stars?

10. What is Bonnie Lynn Raitt's birth name?

The answers are as follows:

1. Cary Grant and Tony Curtis. The film was directed by Blake Edwards. In the ABC-TV adaptation of *Operation Petticoat*, which ran from 1977–1979, Jamie Lee Curtis, daughter of Tony Curtis and Janet Leigh, played the role of Lieutenant Duran. Born William Blake Crump, Blake Edwards, who also directed *Breakfast at Tiffany's*, *The Days of Wine and Roses*, and the *Pink Panther* movies, to name some of his better known films, was married to Julie Andrews from 1969 until his death in 2010.

By the way, Cary Grant and Tony Curtis were also successful in their careers.

2. Gene Wilder, Mel Brooks, and Anne Bancroft.

Gene Wilder's successes included his collaboration with Mel Brooks and much more. Wilder starred in *Willie Wonka and the Chocolate Factory*. He also teamed up with Richard Pryor in four films. The most successful were *Silver Streak* and *Stir Crazy*. *Stir Crazy* was directed by Sidney Portier, who also directed *Hanky Panky*. Wilder met Gilda Radner when they were filming *Hanky Panky*. The two fell in love, and they were later married from 1984 to 1989, when Gilda died of ovarian cancer.

Gilda Radner was flat out funny. If you are not familiar with Gilda, I suggest you spend an hour with her on YouTube. Mel Brooks is a man of many talents. There is a wealth of information about him online. Of course, there is a wealth of information about any celebrity online. So here are a few things you probably don't know about him. During World War II, he defused land mines. Like Kit Carson and Billy Joel, he stands about 5'5". He is one of those rare artists who has won an Emmy, a Grammy, an Oscar, and a Tony—an EGOT.

Mel Brooks and Anne Bancroft were married for almost forty-one years until she passed away in 2005.

Anne Bancroft enjoyed a long and successful career.

In her most recognized role, she played Mrs. Robinson in *The Graduate*. In a way, this is unfortunate because it diverts attention from some of her other excellent work. For example, she won the Academy Award for Best Actress in 1963 for her role as Anne Sullivan in *The Miracle Worker*, which was the story of Helen Keller. Bancroft had four other Academy Award nominations for Best Actress in *The Pumpkin Eater*, *The Turning Point*, *Agnes of God*, and yes, *The Graduate*.

3. Tina Turner, Cher, and Elton John

Some facts you might not know about them—Anna Mae Bullock was born in Nutbush, Tennessee, on November 26, 1939. The 1993 film *What's Love Got to Do with It?* is based on part of Tina's life. We know that Ike Turner repeatedly abused Tina and she survived.

In my humble opinion—and in the opinions of millions of fans, she is not only a diva—she's an icon.

In 2013, Tina married Erwin Bach, a very successful music producer. They have been together since 1985, and they live in Zurich, Switzerland.

Cher was a backup singer for the Phil Spector produced recordings the Ronettes's "Be My Baby" and the Righteous Brothers' "You've Lost That Lovin' Feelin'." Veronica "Ronnie" Bennett was one of the Ronettes. She and Phil Spector were married from approx 1968 to 1974. She still goes by the name Ronnie Spector.

Before they were known as Sonny and Cher, this famous duo performed as Caesar and Cleo.

In 1988, Cher won an Oscar for Best Actress in *Moonstruck*. Olympia Dukakis won the Oscar for Best Supporting Actress in the same movie.

Olympia Dukakis and Michael Dukakis, who was the losing Democratic candidate for U.S. president in 1988, are first cousins. 1988 was a good year for Olympia, not so good for Mike.

I almost forgot to write a few words about Elton John. Sorry, Sir Elton. Certainly one of the great songwriters and showmen of our time. Flamboyant. Controversial.

One of my favorite Elton John songs is "Don't Go Breakin' My Heart," which he sang with KiKi Dee. It's probably not one of his best, but there's a certain charm to it that has always struck a chord with me.

For many years, Elton John has worked to raise millions of dollars/pounds for treatment of people with HIV/AIDS, to promote awareness and prevention of HIV/AIDS, and to combat prejudice against victims of these diseases.

4. Whoopi Goldberg and Demi Moore.

Demi Moore has beauty and talent. Her life is interesting, and at times, it has been difficult, and she might be one of those people who survive and become strong because of the obstacles in life that she has faced. Whoopi Goldberg has achieved her success with a combination of talent, hard work, and personality. She is also an EGOT winner.

Her Oscar was for her role as Oda Mae Brown in *Ghost*. She was nominated by the academy for Best Actress for her role in *The Color*

Purple. The Oscar went to Geraldine Page for *The Trip to Bountiful.* The other three actresses who did not "win" were Anne Bancroft (*Agnes of God*), Jessica Lange (*Sweet Dreams*), and Meryl Streep (*Out of Africa*). These were 1985 films with awards presented in 1986. What a great year for films. Then again, for those of us who love movies, every year is a great year for films.

You can see Whoopi almost every weekday on *The View.* She's the lead hostess.

Oprah Winfrey was nominated for Best Supporting Actress in *The Color Purple.* An outstanding performance. And now I will tell you about Oprah and me.

In the late 1980s, I worked in Chicago and lived in South Bend, Indiana. During the work week, I stayed at my Uncle Barry's condo in Water Tower. Friday after work, I drove home to be with Theo and our children for the weekend. Oprah's Chicago residence was in Water Tower. Her condo was one floor directly over Uncle Barry's. I saw Oprah on a number of occasions, usually in the mornings. I always said hello or good morning. She always responded. And one evening she gave Uncle Barry and me directions to Shaw's Crab House in Chicago. And now you know everything there is to know about my relationship with Oprah. What were you expecting? Although I'm laughing at myself, I have great respect for everything that Oprah has accomplished. She is an amazing person.

Before leaving this long-winded response to Question 4, I want to say something about the "Meryl Streep Phenomenon." In my opinion and in the opinion of many folks who know much more than I, Meryl Streep is our best and most versatile actress. She has won three Oscars as Best Actress or Best Supporting Actress. She has been nominated eighteen times, and she could have and perhaps should have been awarded the Oscar more than three times. Generally speaking, the Oscar nominees are all excellent, and there are many factors that play into determining the Oscar winners.

Meryl Streep is a great actress and a wonderful lady. And Patrick Swayze? Probably best known for his roles in *Ghost, Red Dawn,* and *Dirty Dancing.* He was only fifty-seven when he died of pancreatic cancer in 2009. Too young, too soon.

5. Ginger Rogers and Fred Astaire starred together in ten movies, mostly in the 1930s. As an actor and a singer, Astaire was okay, certainly not great, but his choreography and dancing were exceptional. Ginger Rogers was the most famous of Astaire's dancing partners on film, but he danced with others, including Leslie Caron, Audrey Hepburn, Cyd Charisse (whose birth name was Tula Ellice Finklea), and Ann Miller (whose birth name was Johnnie Lucille Collier).

In addition to being a wonderful dancer, Ginger Rogers was also a good actress. In 1941, she won the Best Actress Oscar for *Kitty Foyle*. By the way, two of her closest friends were Lucille Ball and Bette Davis. Davis was a rival for the 1941 Academy Award for her role in *The Letter*.

If you have never seen Rogers and Astaire dance together, I encourage you to rent a DVD or pick one up at the library. Or find them on YouTube! Great entertainment.

6. George Burns and Jack Benny were best friends. Both started in vaudeville and had successful careers in radio and TV. George Burns made several well-known films, even into his eighties.

In 1977, he starred in *Oh, God!* with the gentleman who is the subject of Celebrity Question 7.

Burns met Gracie Allen in 1922, and they worked as Burns and Allen until 1958 when Gracie retired because of poor health. They married in 1926.

When they first started the act, Gracie was the "straight man," but she was getting so many laughs that they made appropriate changes. Gracie died in 1964. Burns died in 1996 at the age of one hundred.

Gracie was born with heterochromia—one eye was blue and one was green.

Jack Benny lived to be eighty, dying in 1974. At Benny's funeral, as Burns started to give a eulogy, he was overcome with emotion and unable to continue speaking.

Some of my favorite memories from childhood were listening to Jack Benny on the radio on Sunday nights. If you know Rochester and Mr. Kitzel, if you know that Jack Benny drove a Maxwell, and if you know that Jack Benny was thirty-nine years old for most of his life and that he kept his money in a subterranean vault, then you are probably no spring chicken.

Benny was married to Mary Livingstone (born Sadie Marks) from 1927 until his death. A few more tidbits of interest—Jack Benny enjoyed a long, long friendship with the Marx Brothers, he actually played the violin quite well, and there is a school in Waukegan, Illinois, named Jack Benny Middle School and their motto is "Home of the '39ers."

7. John Denver. Theo and I saw him perform in the late '70s or early '80s at the Notre Dame Athletic and Convocation Center, renamed the Joyce Center in 1987 in honor of Rev. Edmund P. Joyce, CSC. Father Ned was the longtime executive VP of Notre Dame, and he worked for some thirty-five years with Father Ted, Rev. Theodore Hesburgh, CSC, STD, president of Notre Dame from 1952 to 1987. After they both retired, the two priests did some traveling together, and Father Hesburgh wrote a book called *Travels with Ted and Ned*.

Why am I rattling on? I was born in South Bend. My parents were born in South Bend. Notre Dame was an important part of my growing up. I was privileged to attend over 150 Notre Dame football games and over three hundred basketball games. And even though it has been years since I lived in South Bend, I still have season tickets for the ND men's basketball team. I buy the tickets and friends reimburse me.

No scalping. I don't believe in it, and Notre Dame doesn't either.

Notre Dame was important for my children as well. We spent hundreds of hours on the soccer fields, on the tennis courts, and at the ice rink on the Notre Dame campus.

Back to John Denver who gave us many great songs that run the emotional gamut from really sad to incredibly joyful. He was an experienced pilot, and he died while flying an experimental plane that was built with flaws, specifically in the location of the fuel gauges—behind the pilot—and the difficulty for the pilot to switch from one fuel tank to the other. On that terrible day, Denver knew both fuel tanks were not full, but he did not intend to fly for very long. Had he taken the time to fuel up both tanks, he might be alive today. One more sad story of a great talent whose life was cut short.

8. Meg Ryan. Most celebrities live interesting lives, and Meg Ryan is no exception. As I read about her professional career, her personal life, and her plastic surgeries, I began to feel sorry for her and other stars who take an absolute beating in the tabloids and online. Nothing is private, and it's hard to know what is true, what is exaggerated, and what is just a bunch of lies. After slogging through a few stories online, I am convinced that I prefer to focus on the successes and the positive accomplishments of Meg Ryan and the other celebrities who interest me.

Tom Hanks has done all right for himself. Some pretty good roles and plenty of talent to play those roles. Consecutive Best Actor Academy Awards for *Philadelphia* and *Forrest Gump*. Think about those two parts—just about as different as two movie roles can possibly be.

9. Buddy Holly, Ritchie Valens, and the Big Bopper. The Big Bopper was suffering from the flu, and he traded places with Waylon Jennings, who was not on the flight. Dion DiMucci, of Dion and the Belmonts, chose not to fly because he didn't want to pay the $36 fee for the flight. Singer/songwriter Don McLean wrote *American Pie*, which is, in part, a tribute to these young singers. When they were about ten and nine years old, my wife, Theo, and "Donnie" lived in the same neighborhood in New Rochelle, New York.

A few years ago, Theo sent him an e-mail, but he did not respond. Perhaps he did not recognize the name "Theo" because he might have known her as "Teddy." Or perhaps he had more important tasks with which to deal. (I deliberately constructed that sentence so you would know that I know a sentence should not end with a preposition.)

I started to write much more about Don McLean and "Starry, Starry Night," but I changed my mind. I'll just mention that Vincent Van Gogh's brother, who was also his best friend, was named Theo.

Let me clarify—Theo Van Gogh was Vincent's best friend, not Don McLean's best friend.

As you have noticed, sometimes I keep writing when I should simply stop. I want this little book to be an easy, enjoyable read, and if I keep typing ad nauseum about every thought that enters my brain, this book could be as big as something written by Tolstoy or Dostoevsky, and you might be deterred from reading it. Then again, you could infer from the title of this book that it was not written by either of those gentlemen. For now, let's agree that both of these incredible authors were long gone before Walmart came along.

10. Bonnie Lynn Raitt. And she is the best. Many artists and athletes are really good, sometimes exceptional, at what they do. And many of them are duds (or worse) as human beings.

I have great admiration for Bonnie Raitt, the musician. And I have great admiration for her as a person. She fought the battles with alcohol and drugs. And she won. For many years she has been aware of many social and political issues, and she has actively participated in "making a difference." Sorry, that is terribly trite, and Bonnie deserves better.

I really, really like her music.

In so many ways, celebrities are just like the rest of us, except that they're famous. They have problems. They have family problems. They have money problems. They have problems with illnesses and addictions. So do we all.

Every celebrity I've written about had setbacks and failures—films that bombed; radio or TV shows that were dropped; records, albums, or CDs that didn't sell well. They've had problems with spouses, boyfriends, girlfriends, parents, and children.

Regular folks have setbacks and failures too. Whether you're famous or not, you're still a human being. And having problems is part of the deal.

In the movie, *The Time Machine*, the Morlocks lead an idyllic life with one fairly major exception. Something about the Eloi. Other than that, they are happy, albeit mindless.

"When the going gets tough, the tough get going" has become a cliché, sometimes humorous, but it's still a pretty good approach.

And Jimmy V's famous "Don't give up...don't ever give up" are words to live by. Enough already.

CHAPTER 5

Where's George

Ninety-six percent of us Americans waste our lives. Four percent achieve something worth noting. These are harsh numbers based on fairly high and extremely subjective standards. (As always, please refer to the short chapter on statistics.) Several questions came to mind as I developed these standards.

When ordinary people do extraordinary things, do they become extraordinary? When extraordinary people do ordinary things, do they go back to being ordinary? Can a person be extraordinary 30 percent of the time, ordinary 60 percent of the time, and underordinary 10 percent of the time? Is underordinary a word? (It is now.) And finally, what does any of this nonsense have to do with George?

As a Walmart cashier, I occasionally find dollar bills stamped, usually in red, with "www.wheresgeorge.com."

This website actually tracks the travels of a dollar bill (or other denominations) as it changes hands. You can go to the website and enter the serial number of the stamped bill and see where the bill has been and when. You can provide info on how you got the bill and where. All the history for the bills is based on input by the participants who have entered over 237,000,000 bills since the website was launched on December 23, 1998.

I first visited wheresgeorge.com on June 20, 2013, and I was overwhelmed by what I saw. And a bit puzzled. Lots of information about paper money, some of it rather interesting. Maps, mileage charts, profiles of people who participate, and much more!

Computer programs have to be pretty good to track all this data. I am puzzled because this incredible collection of data is useless to most people, certainly to me. Once you track a couple of bills and find out that a specific dollar bill traveled 6,238 miles in 489 days, the novelty wears off. I don't want to know about hundreds or thousands of bills.

I'm sure some folks spend an hour or more a day on the wheresgeorge.com website. The most frequent users are recognized and listed, along with the number of bills they have put into the system. I think it's a waste of time, but in fairness, those frequent users would probably think I'm wasting too much time listening to and watching baseball. There are millions of baseball fans. Wheresgeorge has thousands of followers and many of them are really into what's going on at their website. For example, a quick check at 9:00 PM Pacific Time shows over 6,500 hits for the day. And 41,000 new bills entered. The most active participant has entered almost 2,200,000 bills. I don't know how many years that took, but he obviously enjoys what he's doing. And if he's happy, I'm happy for him.

There are online stores too—the Old George Store and the Where's George Premium Store. You can buy Where's George T-shirts, buttons, coasters, stickers, mugs, etc.

So how are you wasting your life? Or are you one of the 4 percent? Hey, I told you at the very beginning that my standards are extremely subjective. And so are yours.

CHAPTER 6

Saga of the Liquor Store

I started working as a cashier in the liquor store in mid-November 2012. Our new store manager, Carolyn, wanted a cashier on duty until 10:30 PM on weeknights and until midnight on weekends during the holiday season. I was the designated cashier for four or five nights a week, depending on my assigned schedule. I don't know why I was chosen, but my guesses are that management knew I was mature and dependable. And very slow in terms of scans per hour. Perhaps they decided to keep the faster cashiers on the belts and the express lanes.

Please keep in mind the liquor store in our Walmart is really small, about 675 square feet. That limits our selection and inventory dramatically compared to a full-line competitor; however, we're really convenient for thousands of customers who plan to be in our store for other shopping.

I looked at this new situation as a challenge even if it turned out to be temporary. It was amusing to me that I was cashiering liquor, wine, and cigarettes because I don't smoke, and I don't drink alcoholic beverages; although I now joke that I've worked at Walmart long enough that I'm ready to start drinking.

(I did smoke part of a pack of cigarettes when I was fifteen. About 9:00 PM on a school night, I told my father that I needed something for school, a notebook or a folder, whatever. Back then, "whatever" was not an expression—I'm saying "whatever" now because I can't remember exactly what I needed from the store fifty-six years ago.

My father did not want to drive me to the store. He told me to walk. I was angry. To pay him back for not driving me to the store, I bought a pack of cigarettes in addition to the whatever. I don't remember what brand I bought. As I recall, the most popular cigarettes then were Camels, Lucky Strikes, and Chesterfields. Camels are still very popular. Lucky Strikes and Chesterfields have almost disappeared from U.S. stores, but they can be purchased online.

Whatever they were, I coughed through a couple of them as I walked home and coughed through a few more over the next day or two. I never did figure out how to inhale without coughing, so I threw away the rest of the pack and decided that I would not smoke again.)

Back to Walmart. Right away, I realized that I had to know enough to be helpful to the customers. I learned that cigarette manufacturers are not allowed to label their products as lights and ultralights. They use colors to designate the strength of the cigarette. Marlboro reds are regular, golds are lights, and silvers are ultralights. Marlboro also sells 27s, 72s, 83s, smooths, blacks, red labels, special blends, nexts, southern cut, edge, a bunch of menthols, and others I can't think of off the top of my head. According to the Philip Morris USA website, Marlboro's market share in 2013 was 43.7 percent, and the Philip Morris USA market share in 2013 was 50.6 percent. They also manufacture Parliament, L&M, Basic, Virginia Slim, Chesterfield cigarettes, and several others as well.

Cigarettes can vary in length. Generally, they range in length from 70 mm to 120 mm. Some are "wides," some are standard, some are ultrathin. To me they are all nasty, and I am especially disappointed when I sell a pack of cigarettes to an eighteen- or nineteen-year-old kid.

Enough about cigarettes. Let's move on to the booze. Learning enough about cigarettes to be competent as a cashier is easy. Depending on the level of expertise one aspires to achieve, learning about wine and liquor can take anywhere from a few hours to a lifetime. I just wanted to know what we sell and where in the store it is located and to know what we don't sell.

After working a few shifts in the liquor store, I made a list on a three-by-five card with all of the empty spots on the shelves where twenty different products were supposed to be. I showed the card to Co-manager John, and he was not happy with our two vendors, Southern Wine and Spirits and Wirtz Beverage Group. John left the liquor store, and within minutes, he was back with Assistant Manager Stacy. The next day they made some phone calls, and they probably scheduled meetings with the vendors. Southern's service improved right away and has continued to be fairly good, but not great. Wirtz's service is still spotty and inconsistent.

This is my take on how the system works. The Walmart associates do not stock the wine and liquor products. The salespeople from the vendors visit the liquor store with their handheld computers. They survey the shelves and supposedly look at the storage areas in the back of the store to make sure they know what is already in stock. Then they order what they perceive to be our needs. The vendors' delivery drivers bring these orders to the store and put them in the storage areas.

The vendors' merchandisers (stockers) take the products from the storage areas and put them on the shelves. The stockers from the two vendors do not always respect each other's storage areas and shelf space. Sometimes they move the inventory around. I've seen stockers take their competitor's bottles off an end cap, a display at the end of an aisle, and put up their own product. This kind of activity happens occasionally, but not often. The merchandisers are busy, they have other stores to service, and they work fast. I rarely see them because they are usually in and out of the store before my shift starts, which is 3:00 PM on most days.

After working a few more shifts in the liquor store, I wrote the following memo and handed it to Co-manager John.

November 22, 2012

Now that I have cashiered the Liquor Store for a whole week, I am an expert with strong opinions about how we can improve this particular part of our Walmart store.

Seriously, I'm no expert, but I do have a few ideas and suggestions to offer. Other departments have managers and sales associates who specialize in what they do; for example, associates in Sporting Goods know a few things about sports and sports equipment. And they know something about manufacturers, pricing, inventory, etc.

By contrast, the cashiers in the liquor store have no particular knowledge about product, quality, competition, or pricing. They just rotate in and out. I suggest that we should manage our liquor store.

1. Maximize sales and minimize lost sales by managing our inventory. We can track l/s sales to determine what sells and what doesn't.

   Vendors have to do a better job of restocking our shelves. Running out of fast-moving items like Franzia box Chardonnay and Merlot or Menage a Trois California Red Wine is unacceptable. We can keep extra stock in the l/s in the same places that overzealous vendors are hiding slower moving items.

2. Specify a handful of cashiers to learn the l/s as a department. Train them to know something about our products—what's the difference between moscato and chardonnay? Between pinot grigio and pinot noir? Keep a simple hand-book with basic information and a few cocktail recipes.

3. Pricing. We should be aware of how our competitors are pricing their products so that we can be competitive. If customers actually start visiting our store to buy their wine and liquor because we offer a good inventory and great prices, they will shop other departments as well.

I have other ideas, but I'll keep this brief. You might be willing to read a page of my thoughts, but not a book.

I hope it's not inappropriate for a cashier to offer input in this way. I've always been outspoken and quite comfortable talking about ways to improve customer service and increase profits. Besides, I'm disappointed that I've been unable to advance so far (two attempts at a CSM position) and bored with regular cashiering. So if some of my ideas can help our Liquor Store, implementing them can also help boost my self-esteem.

Respectfully submitted,
Ronn Medow

Two weeks later, Co-manager John was in the liquor store to buy a pack of cigarettes. He said, "I read your letter. It had some good ideas. I'll be talking to (store manager) Carolyn in a day or two to see if we can make some changes."

Another three weeks went by and there was no further communication. The word "dysfunctional" popped into my brain. But wait—there's more!

On December 29, I dropped a second memo addressed to Carolyn into the suggestion box. The second memo was attached to the first memo.

Here is the second memo, verbatim, except for the name changes of the managers.

12-29-2012

Dear Carolyn,

Having worked my shifts in the liquor store during the holiday season, I've talked to and listened to hundreds of customers. And listening to the customers and responding to their requests is how we build a better business.

Based on our customers' input and my observations, I offer the following suggestions:

1. We should stock sherry and port wines, ouzo, cocktail onions, maraschino cherries, and hot buttered rum mix. We can take the chewing gum, beef jerky, batteries, and chocolate bars out—they do not sell.

2. We have 3 slow moving products, all from Wirtz, that take up way too much shelf space. We can reduce out inventories of Fetzer wines, Camarena tequila, and Madria sangria and use the valuable space gained to stock better selling products.

3. Cigarettes—customers rarely buy soft packs.

    When they do, it's usually because we are out of the box packs. Why don't we get rid of soft packs? We can save time and handling, not have to deal with so much out of date product. The cigarette racks are in poor condition. Many need replacement or repair.

4. Improve "in-house" supply to the L/S. We're often out of bloody mary mix,

Angostura bitters, Rose's grenadine, and various mixers. Empty shelves=lost sales. This is an easy fix.

5. Periodically check Costco, Ben's, and other competitors' prices. Price product to sell, not to sit on shelves.

6. Fix the Sensormatic.

7. Scrub the floor on a regular basis. Nightly sweeping is not sufficient.

I don't want to cause problems or throw anyone under the bus—just want to take good care of our customers and make the L/S a well-run profit center.

Enclosed is a letter I gave to Co-Mgr John on 11-22-12.

Sincerely,
Ronn Medow
Cashier

A number of products, including some electronics, some DVDs, expensive perfume, etc., at Walmart have a security tag attached to them. If a customer or a thief takes the product through the exit without having had the security tag "demagnetized," the system sets off a chime and a spoken electronic message to tell the customer and the Walmart associates that something of value is going out the door.

Sensormatic is the name of the company that makes our electronic surveillance equipment. And I use that word to describe the "demagnetizer" that is adjacent to each cash register.

I did not hear a word for several weeks, and I wrote a short note to Carolyn.

Dear Carolyn,

On December 29, I put a letter to you in the locked suggestion box. Attached to the letter was a previous letter from November 22nd that I had handed to Co-Mgr John.

I'm wondering whether you ever saw these letters or were they perhaps intercepted and not given to you? Thanks in advance for letting me know.

Sincerely,
Ronn Medow
Cashier

02-14-2013
Happy Valentine's Day!

Two more weeks passed. No communication. No response. On February 28, I clocked in and saw that Carolyn was in the managers' office. I asked her if she had received my letters. She said she had given them to Asst. Manager Flo. Then she complimented me on her father's experience when he made a purchase in the liquor store. I didn't know her father, and he didn't say, "By the way, I'm Carolyn's dad." I liked hearing the kind words, and once again I was reminded that you don't always know who you are talking to, so it's important to be friendly and professional with every customer. Every customer. Every time. (Not just at Walmart—at any job in which you deal with customers, face-to-face or on the phone or online.)

Still, I was puzzled. Why did Carolyn or Assistant Manager Flo never acknowledge the letters? I hope you can sense my level of frustration and bewilderment. I'm not used to offering input and receiving no response whatsoever. Even a negative response is a response.

When you read the chapter called "Thinking Inside the Box," you will see my effort to summarize the thinking that Walmart encourages. Of course, my work experience at Walmart has been confined to only one store. There are thousands of Walmart stores. Are they all basically the same? Or are there stores where management encourages associates to put forth ideas and suggestions?

Thinking that maybe Carolyn did not want to deal with a cashier, someone too many levels below her, I approached two brand-new co-managers who were brought in to be part of Carolyn's team. They were kind enough to give me an hour of their time, but with all the interruptions, it was really more like half an hour. I gave each of them copies of my letters, and they were receptive to my ideas and concerns.

Sorry to tell you the bottom line—there were so many problems to deal with throughout the entire store that the liquor store was simply not a high priority. Profit margins in the liquor store are about 12 percent. Walmart makes more money on four pounds of bananas than it makes on a $12 bottle of wine or liquor.

So the ideas and suggestions for the liquor store would just have to wait. When I asked why we couldn't work on several "projects" at the same time, they explained that management was already stretched too thin.

Then what I hoped would be a breakthrough took place. In October of 2013, Beth went from being a customer service manager to the department manager for Dept 82, a difficult and thankless job. This was more of a lateral move than a promotion. Beth was responsible for cigarettes, wine and liquor, candy and gum, and possibly more that I'm not aware of. Candy is huge. There are displays at every register. I was pleased for Beth; we got along well, and she had always been very nice to me.

Beth's first day as department manager was Monday, October 7, 2013. I did not see her until Friday, October 18. I congratulated her, wished her well, and told her I had a number of ideas to improve the liquor store. Half teasing, half serious, I promised to make her "look good."

We talked about our schedules and the only times our workdays coincided were Thursday and Friday. And her shift was usually over by the time I started my shift. Hoping for an hour of overlap, we agreed to talk on Thursday or Friday, October 24 and 25. When I arrived at work on October 24, Beth was gone. She had to leave early because of a situation at school involving one of her children. I did not see her on the 25. She had taken the day off.

And so it went for weeks. I finally left copies of the letters to management dated 11-22-12 and 12-29-12 for Beth, and I scribbled a few notes.

She received them! And one good result came from one of the notes. I had recommended that we stock plenty of champagne during the holiday season because we had run out of so many champagnes in 2012. For November and December of 2013, we did not run out of champagne. Life's little victories!

Now it's February 2014. Beth has left Walmart to pursue a different career path. I wish her well; although I've seen her only five times since last October. Sometimes just a "Hi, Beth."

The liquor store inventory is still way out of balance, way too much slow-moving inventory, and always running out of faster-moving inventory.

Empty shelves still equal lost sales. Our cigarette inventory is a disaster. The two best-selling cigarettes are Marlboro Reds and Marlboro Golds, both in a box, not a soft pack. I have not seen Reds or Golds for at least four days. I don't know who is ordering cigarettes. Evidently, nobody.

I am still the only cashier who knows anything about the liquor store, what we carry, what we don't carry, where everything is or is supposed to be.

We still do not sell sherry, port, marsala, ouzo, or hot buttered rum mix. The store is never clean enough to suit me. Every shift, I spend some time dusting the shelves and bottles. Sometimes I wash the shelves with soap and water. We do have maintenance people who sweep the floors, but the area behind the cash register is not pretty. It always needs scrubbing.

The situation in the liquor store has frustrated me for a year and a half. In the great scheme of things, it's not important. But I do spend a number of hours every week working here, so I'm disappointed that I have been completely ineffective at making any improvements.

CHAPTER 7

Go-Backs

Until I started working at "my" Walmart store in Reno, I had seldom walked into any Walmart store anywhere.

Too huge, almost intimidating. Too hard to find what I wanted. Now I've been working in the same store for three years, and I still can't find much of what I want, let alone help the customers find what they want.

Putting go-backs away takes me forever, partly because when I finally arrive at the proper place to put back the go-back, I find a half dozen other items out of place, so those items then become go-backs.

Give me a whole shopping cart full of go-backs and I might be gone for days at a time. "Have you seen Ronn?"

"Saw him about an hour ago putting back towels and washcloths. He had a crazed look on his face. Desperate. And his canteen was out of water."

Fortunately, I'm usually working at a cash register, and putting go-backs away is only an occasional task for me. Occasional, but daunting. You may recall that I'm easily daunted.

CHAPTER 8

Walmart Stories II: Liquor Store

These little stories all happened while I was cashiering in the liquor store.

1. Cashier Lulu loves to talk and joke with the customers. Sometimes she's way out there and she is not a good listener.

She was breaking me—that is, she took over my register while I went on a break. Returning to the liquor store, I overheard this conversation as Lulu and a lady customer completed their transaction.

Customer: "I'm celebrating. I just finished in court. I'm so glad it's finally over. Fighting with my husband and his lawyer."

Lulu: "I had five husbands, and I killed all of them."

Customer: "That's why I was in court. My husband accused me of trying to kill him."

Lulu: "I stabbed them. Now I'm looking for number 6. Thank you for shopping at Walmart."

The customer took her bags and left. Lulu signed off the register.

I asked Lulu, "Did you hear what she was telling you?"

"No. What did she say?"

"She was in court because her husband accused her of trying to murder him."

"Oh my," said Lulu. As she walked out of the liquor store, Lulu said to me, "If I don't like number 6, I'll cut off his ding dong."

I called out to her, "Then I'll make sure I'm not number 6."

A few weeks later, Lulu asked me if I remembered the incident. She said she had dreamed that she was being held as a prisoner for encouraging the customer to kill her husband. I was in the dream, pointing at Lulu and saying that she was guilty. Lulu said she was angry at me for betraying her and making the accusations.

Lulu is a character and sometimes she's flaky, but she has a heart of gold. She often buys snacks and gifts for other associates. At my register she once bought a snack and requested $100 cash back on her debit card.

She gave the snack and the money to an associate who was going through some difficult times.

2. While I was waiting on a customer, Cashier Gert walked into the liquor store to break me. The customer looked at Gert and said, "Excuse me. You have a bunch of toilet paper hanging out of your pants."

"Oh, how embarrassing," said Gert. "But thank you for telling me."

As Gert was cleaning up her act, so to speak, I was very busy with my cash register. I didn't want to make eye contact with Gert for fear of adding to her embarrassment.

The customer said, "I always tell people what I think. If you walked in with a booger hanging out of your nose, I'd tell you that too. It's better to say something than let a person walk around like that."

I handed the customer his receipt and his change. "Thank you, sir. Hope you enjoy your day."

As he left the counter, he said, "I will. I enjoy every day."

I signed off the register. "Thanks, Gert. I'll be back in fifteen minutes."

3. When parents are shopping at the liquor store and they have children with them, sometimes the parents instruct the children to stand just outside and sometimes the kids come into the liquor store. There are no doors. The store is just an alcove that opens out to the main store.

One day a little girl about seven years old was standing next to her mother in front of the register. I asked the mother for an ID—our procedure is to card anyone who is buying tobacco or alcoholic beverages if he or she appears to be forty or younger. The mother showed me her driver's license. As I was ringing up the sale, I leaned over the counter and asked the little girl, "Are you twenty-one?"

The seven-year-old didn't miss a beat. She fired back, "I am twenty-one, but I'm very short for my age!"

4. As I was scanning barcodes on several bottles, I overheard part of a conversation among four adults. Two of them appeared to be siblings. They were talking about their Christmas gifts. One of them said, "Grandma gave us an electric turkey fryer. What in the hell am I going to do with an electric turkey fryer?"

I suggested, "Fry electric turkeys?"

5. I have a regular customer I call the Weatherman. He starts talking to me as he approaches the register. He always buys a six-pack, and he always talks about the weather. Nonstop. I hardly say a word. Don't have to.

Just say thank-you before he leaves, still talking. He stopped by on Good Friday, almost distraught. "We've got a beautiful day today. Sunshine. Temperature is 72. But by Easter, it'll be colder, and we'll have weather. Why does it always rain on Easter? It's so frustrating."

By the way, back in Indiana we had weather every day, sometimes good, sometimes not so good. In Reno, "weather" means rain or snow. Interesting little tidbit.

6. I saw a $10 bill lying on the floor in front of my register. I picked it up and gave it to Customer Service Manager Mary Jane.

She put the ten in an envelope and left it at the customer service counter. If anyone claimed it, we would give him or her the $10. If no one claimed it, we would contribute it to the Children's Miracle Network, one of Walmart's favorite charity projects. (Many disparaging words have been written and spoken about Walmart, but please think about this: Since 1987, Walmart and Sam's Club customers, associates, and members in United States and Canada have raised more than $650 million for CMN, including $64 million in 2012. For more information please visit www.childrensmiraclenetwork.org and www.walmartfoundation.org.)

About two hours later, a young man approached me at my register and asked if anyone had found a $10 bill. I recognized him from his previous visit. We retrieved the money from the customer service counter, and the young man was both happy and relieved. I was pleased that everything went right and thought about the odds that someone could drop a ten in a Walmart store in Reno and eventually get the money back. My guess is two out of one hundred.

7. A lady visited the liquor store and asked me if we carried Porta Vita. I confessed that I was not familiar with it and asked where she had seen it. "Oh," she said, "I had it at the Eye-talian restaurant on Kietzke." "Italian restaurant on Kietzke?" I asked, trying to picture an Italian restaurant on Kietzke Lane in Reno.

Then she remembered. "Olive Garden!"

Well, I thought it was funny.

When I got home, I went online. Sure enough, Olive Garden's signature wines are the Porta Vita Collection.

8. An older man and a little girl, perhaps grandfather and granddaughter, walked into the liquor store. The girl, about nine years old, asked, "Why do you always have to get drunk?"

The grandfather muttered something I could not hear, pulled a bottle from the shelf, and the two left the store. Sorry, I can't tell you that the bottle was Old Granddad, but it might have been Early Times or Ancient Age.

9. My customer, a "regular," said, "My wife's out of town. I can sit naked in the leather chair and fart all day, and she can't object."

Unable to think of anything better to say, I asked, "To what would she object? The naked part or the farting part?"

The customer replied, "What you said."

10. I asked the customer for her ID, and she said, "You've done me before."

Many possible replies, none of them appropriate, raced through my mind. I could feel my face heat up, and I was blushing.

Immediately, of course, she realized what she had said, and I tried to smooth away the awkward moment by saying, "Yes, I've waited on you before."

It was almost a flirtatious moment, but it wasn't. It was 98 percent innocent and 2 percent not innocent. It was funny and uncomfortable at the same time. And that's all I have to say about that.

CHAPTER 9

Carmen

When I started working at Walmart, I met Carmen, who was a Walmart associate. Actually, you don't really meet each other. It's more accurate to say you become aware of each other. On a given day, you work on a register near someone. You read the name badge and the name may or may not stay in your memory the first time or two. Or an associate may stop at your register to purchase a few items or a cartful of groceries or clothes, etc.

And we make small talk. How's your day? Working late today? It's your Friday—that's good. So one day I asked Carmen, who was bright and personable and in her early twenties, if she also went to school, meaning college. She told me she had quit.

Did she plan to build a career at Walmart? No, she was just killing time, not sure what she wanted to do. She should go back to school, she said, but she's too lazy.

An old person like me could not let this pass—an opportunity to offer "sage" advice, wanted or not. Life goes by day by day. Killing time is wasting time, and most of us waste so much time, we end up wasting our lives.

Carmen, if you weren't so lazy, what would you be interested in doing? Do you have a passion for something, something you really care about?

I like animals. I might want to work with animals. Perfect, I joked. Maybe Walmart *is* the place for you. We had short conversations over the next few weeks—one, two, five minutes squeezed in during overlapping breaks or when meeting by chance somewhere in the store. I always encouraged her to make a commitment. To herself. To make her life better. To do something she really loved to do.

One day, Carmen told me she had given notice, and she was moving back to California and going back to school. On her last day at Walmart, she said good-bye and gave me a hug.

About a year later, Carmen was in Reno, and she stopped by the store. I was working on a register, slammed, and she gave me another hug.

"Are you happy?" I asked.

She smiled. "Yes."

I was sorry I couldn't stop and talk, even for a minute. Can't keep our customers waiting.

Thinking about Carmen from time to time, I hope I helped her to make a good decision, maybe even a lasting commitment.

It's not likely that I'll ever know.

CHAPTER 10

Asset Protection

It's 4:20 AM as I sit and type. Yesterday, I started my shift at 2:00 PM. One glance at the liquor store and I saw that the cigarettes were not shelved. At register 17 (subsequently changed to register 13 after eight new self-check registers were installed to replace the four self-checks we used to have), we have a complete tobacco shop—cigarettes, cigars, chewing tobacco, electronic cigarettes, etc.

Behind the register is a secure area. Nobody can get into the area without walking through a little gate right next to the cash register and the cashier. This area also houses our podium, a small platform the customer service managers use as a headquarters. The platform has locking drawers where we keep the money for supplying the cash registers with sufficient cash and change. Register 17 is open 24-7.

Normally, every morning, the cashier who "opens" the liquor store rolls the shopping carts with the cigarettes into the alcove that is our liquor store and puts the cigarette racks onto the shelves behind the counter.

Just cigarettes—packs and a few cartons. And normally, every evening, the cashier who "closes" the liquor store pulls the racks from the shelves and puts them into shopping carts to take the cigarettes back to the secure area behind register 17.

If the cigarettes are shelved in the liquor store, there is a cashier on duty. If not, then no cashier. The liquor store doesn't really open and close. Customers always have access to it. If no cashier is on duty there, the customer takes his or her items to any register, even self-check.

So yesterday as I started my shift, I was told by a customer service manager that someone had decided that today we were not "opening" the liquor store.

This decision seemed odd because yesterday was a Friday, and the two busiest days in the liquor store are Friday and Saturday. The anonymous decision maker must have determined that we needed more manpower or womanpower on the regular registers.

I was assigned to work at register 15, a long belt with no restriction on the number of items a customer can purchase. If I can't be in the liquor store, I much prefer working at an express lane register where, theoretically, the limit is twenty items.

Just before I went to register 15, I walked through the liquor store to check the shelves, which were in complete disarray. Of course, as the day wore on, the disarray became a total mess. So idiot that I am, I was upset. Nobody cares that the shelves in the liquor store are messy. But I do.

Being upset about the messy shelves is not why I am writing at this hour instead of sleeping. Here is the reason I am upset. About 7:40 PM I was returning to work after lunch. I approached Customer Service Manager Courtney to ask her if I could move to an express lane since I saw that we had only one express lane open.

Courtney was talking through her headphones to the asset protection assistant. A young man with a cartload of merchandise had just wheeled the cart out of the store without paying. I should have gone to a register to resume working, but I walked with Courtney to the grocery side entrance. The asset protection assistant was standing in front of the store, and the three of us watched as the culprit wheeled the cart to his vehicle in the Jack-in-the-Box parking lot across from the Walmart parking lot.

Let me backtrack for a moment. Maybe a year or so ago, the people greeters in our store were taken off the doors and given other duties. They chase down stray carts and shopping baskets. They help customers find departments. They put away go-backs.

We observed from this change that our "shrinkage" increased dramatically. Shrinkage is mostly theft, but according to one of our managers, some of it comes from not taking write downs in a timely manner. Our April 2012 inventory showed a shrinkage of approximately $439,000. Our April 2013 inventory showed shrinkage of over $900,000. And I heard, but cannot verify, that our April 2014 inventory showed shrinkage of $1.6 million. Maybe some of it is in accounting procedures, but an awful lot of it is theft. Even sixty-five- and seventy-year-old people greeters are a deterrent to theft, but they were assigned to other duties.

Another reason for this ridiculous, embarrassingly high amount of theft is our procedure. If a Walmart associate observes a customer who might be trying to steal from us, said associate is to find a salaried manager or the asset protection manager or the asset protection assistant. We are very restricted as to what we can say to the suspect. We cannot apprehend him/her. We can practice "aggressive customer service" by asking the "customer" if we can be of assistance or if we can help the "customer" find an available cashier.

Talking to a customer sometimes makes him/her aware that we know he/she is there. It might make the customer have second thoughts about stealing. Many times we have seen a customer "give up" and abandon a shopping cart filled with items he/she intended to steal. Alas, many times the culprit succeeds with the theft.

If we can't get an authorized "apprehender" in front of the suspected thief within thirty seconds or less, the theft is usually a done deal. And these managers and asset protection people are not that easy to find.

So I'm upset to the point of having a difficult night. I'm upset because the asset protection assistant became a spectator and did not do her job.

While I'm ranting about this incident, let me recall another situation I discovered under the direction of our previous managers. One night I waited on a customer service associate from another store. She was buying a couple of electric toothbrushes and she gave me a $7 manufacturer's coupon and a $10 manufacturer's coupon.

A few minutes after we completed our transaction, I saw her at the customer service counter. I walked up close to find out if there was an issue. Did I make a mistake? Was she dissatisfied?

I learned that she was returning the items she had just bought for full credit, enabling her to pocket the $17 from the two coupons. I complained to Customer Service Manager Courtney, "She used coupons to buy those items. It's dishonest. It's cheating."

Courtney said it was okay because Walmart did not lose any money. I went to the asset protection manager at the time, Ralph, and he agreed with Courtney. "Walmart submits the coupons to the manufacturer for redemption, and we don't get hurt. " "But when we submit the coupons to the manufacturer," I protested, "we're misrepresenting."

"Technically, no," said Ralph. "At the time of the purchase, the customer submitted the coupons to us." Here I was, outraged over an incident that cashiers are not even supposed to think about, let alone worry about. So at that time, nothing changed.

A few weeks later, Lisa, one of our own associates, tried to do a similar trick at my register. She was buying three electric toothbrushes and handed me three $7 coupons.

I called over a customer service manager, Courtney again, and said discreetly, "I don't know exactly what Lisa plans to do, but something isn't right."

Courtney told Lisa that she could buy only one electric toothbrush and use only one coupon.

I mentioned the incident to Ralph. Within two days, notices were posted by both the time clocks to the effect that this coupon scam was dishonest and associates were not allowed to continue doing it. Effective immediately.

No one said a word to me—Ralph, salaried managers, customer service managers—not a word, but I would like to think that my objections played a part in getting this policy changed.

It could go without saying, but I'll say it anyway, that 97 percent of the customers are 88 percent honest. And the mostly honest customers pay for the acts of the dishonest by paying higher prices. Imagine, if we had 100 percent honesty, Walmart's low, low prices would be even lower!

As I write this particular paragraph, it's early January 2014. A few nights ago, our "new" asset protection manager, Leo, who replaced Ralph, was standing at the "grocery" entrance with another associate, a woman I do not know. The "gm" (general merchandise) entrance/exit was blocked off with shopping carts and an associate standing guard. Leo and the associate were checking receipts to make sure that people leaving the store had actually paid for their purchases. What a great idea! At this point, our store had not followed this procedure for perhaps a year and a half. I volunteered my opinion that we should check all receipts 24-7. Our Costco store checks all receipts and Costco shoppers don't seem to be offended.

I asked Leo if we were going to continue doing this. His answer was noncommittal.

So now, as I write this particular paragraph, it is April 2014. I'm putting the finishing touches on my manuscript. Leo is no longer working at our store, and we do not check the customers' receipts.

One more thought about the self-check registers. Walmart knows that a considerable amount of theft takes place at the self-checks. Walmart also knows that more self check stations = fewer cashier hours. Evidently, the amount of money Walmart saves by paying cashiers less is more than the amount of "shrinkage" suffered at the self-checks.

And so it goes.

CHAPTER 11

Walnut Stories III: Liquor Store

1. A young man wanted to buy a handle—a 1.75 liter bottle of liquor. I checked his ID, and he was of legal age. Then he said, "Before I buy this, can I do one thing?"

"What's that?" I asked.

"I want to see if I can sneak this into a movie," he said. And he pushed the bottle down into the front of his pants.

"Yeah, that'll work," he said.

I gave him a couple of plastic bags so he could do his own bagging.

"Well," I said, "you are definitely going to impress your friends when you walk into that theater."

2. A customer was buying a bottle of Skye vodka. As I was putting the bottle in a paper bag, then a plastic bag, the bottle slipped, and I caught it before it fell off the counter.

"Wow," I remarked, "for a second there, we could say, 'The Skye is falling.'"

3. We have various codes to identify emergency situations. For example, Code Adam means there is a missing child. Code Red means there is a fire. Code Brown means there is a shooting situation.

One day just outside the liquor store, Customer Service Manager Courtney was standing next to some human or pet feces on the floor. There was an orange hazard cone, but Courtney was directing traffic, making sure that nobody accidently stepped in the feces. It seemed to take the maintenance people a long time to respond. (I couldn't imagine why.)

I said to Courtney, "This gives a whole new meaning to Code Brown."

4. In the liquor store, we feature liquor, wine, and cigarettes; but we can scan and cashier anything as long as it is not produce that has to be weighed. There is no scale. I was explaining this situation to a customer, and I joked that Walmart would not let me guess how much the produce weighed, even though I was confident that I could guess weights within two pounds. For produce. The customer misunderstood. He said, "All right. How much do I weigh?"

I looked at him and said, "One fifty-nine."

He was amazed. I had guessed his exact weight. A few weeks later, the same customer was in the liquor store with his son. He was telling the boy that I was the guy who had guessed his weight.

The father asked, "How much does my son weigh?"

I looked at the son and said, "Seventy-seven pounds."

The father asked his son, 'What do you weigh?"

"Seventy-six," said the boy.

I'm thinking about leaving Walmart and running away to the carnival.

5. A sad story. A father and daughter visited the liquor store. The girl was eleven or twelve. She and her father were arguing about the size of

the bottle he was going to buy. The father put a handle of vodka on the counter. The girl took the bottle off the counter and returned it to the shelf. She insisted that her father buy a smaller bottle. He threatened to return the doll and the video game he had just bought for her, and he retrieved the handle and put it back on the counter. We completed the transaction, the father pushed his shopping cart out of the liquor store, and the daughter threw herself down on the floor. She sat against a wine display with her knees pulled up to her chest and her arms crossed. After about thirty seconds of pouting, she got up and followed her father out of the store.

I don't know why she was so upset about her father's buying the bigger bottle. There are several possible reasons, and most of them are not things that I want to think about.

6. Associate Phyliss visited the liquor store and asked me if the L&M Turkish Blends and Turkish Nights were on sale. I did not know. I did not remember ever selling a pack. I scanned a pack, and sure enough, they were priced in the computer at a closeout price of $1.87 per pack plus tax, even though the price on the shelves was over $5.

There were eight Blends and ten Nights, and Phyliss bought all of them. She mentioned the cigarettes were not for her. In my semiper-manent state of confusion—I was wondering how she knew they were on closeout—I blurted out something like, "They're not for you?"

"No," she said. "I sell them to my roommate for $4 a pack."

As Phyliss left the liquor store, I asked myself, "Self, what is the unusual nature of Phyliss's relationship with her roommate? "

Self had no answers.

7. Two kids, a boy and a girl about seven and eight years old, came into the liquor store with their father. They had just bought noodles, foam noodles used as toys and flotation devices in swimming pools. Out of the water, the noodles can be used as pugil sticks, and the kids started hitting each other as their father was making his purchase. In my opinion, a liquor store is not a good place to have a noodle fight. Before their father told them to stop, they knocked only one bottle off

the shelf. The bottle did not break. Could have been a small disaster. Turned out OK.

8. Walmart's policy is to ask purchasers of tobacco and alcoholic beverages for an ID if the purchaser appears to be forty or younger. In many cases, I glance at the photo and look at the birth date. If the purchaser looks really young, I look at the ID more carefully. I check the height and weight shown on the ID against the appearance of the customer.

Sometimes the customers have grown taller or gained or lost weight since the ID, usually a driver's license, was issued.

One experience involved a young woman whose license said she was five feet eight inches tall and weighed 150. She appeared to be about five two and 125. My mind, like a steel trap, started calculating. She could have lost twenty-five pounds and that could affect her face, which was not like the photo on the license, but why did she look so short?

I stood on my tiptoes and leaned over the counter—I was thinking she might have really low heels on her shoes. Or maybe she was standing in a depression in the floor. There's so much talk about the economy—recession, depression, etc.

Finally I decided that this license was not really hers. I hate confrontations, but now was the time for me to be gently assertive. "I'm sorry," I said. "I can't sell you this bottle of wine. This license is not yours."

She smiled, resigned. "I know."

9. Many, many women lie about their weight. Or else they gain lots of pounds after the driver's license is issued. Men will occasionally trim ten or thirty pounds off their real weight at the DMV.

Women are shameless. Of course, I never say a word, but it's commonplace to see licenses that say a woman is 5'5" and 135 pounds, and I know she's 170 or 190 or 210 or whatever.

I did see an ID for one young woman whose license said she was 5'4" and 348 pounds. An honest woman.

I'll say more about weight and obesity in the next chapter, which is called "You Are What You Eat."

10. A young woman put a bottle of wine and two cans of tomato paste on the counter. I said, "May I please see an ID? Whenever you buy tomato paste, we have to ask for an ID."

"Really?" she asked before she realized that I was joking.

"Yes," I replied. "Walmart has lots of rules about tomato paste."

CHAPTER 12

You Are What You Eat

One of the most striking experiences at Walmart is seeing the large number of people who are overweight or fat or obese. Or morbidly obese. Both customers and Walmart Associates. Every day I see people using shopping carts to support their weight as they walk through the store.

When I cashier their groceries, I am usually appalled at seeing what they buy—too much candy, bags and bags of potato chips and tortilla chips, packages of cookies, doughnuts galore, countless cans and bottles and multipacks of soda, ice cream, frozen dinners, especially pizzas, and food in cans. So many empty calories, calories without nutrition. Not enough fresh fruits and vegetables.

Only once do I remember talking to an obese person about weight. I am not comfortable initiating such a conversation, but it's something I think about. My perception is that, with some exceptions, being overweight is a choice. And I do not understand why so many folks choose to live their lives carrying around so much weight. Maybe they're just overwhelmed by the challenge of losing a large number of pounds.

Certainly this example is oversimplified. Let's say Joseph weighs 290 pounds, and he would like to lose seventy pounds. In Joseph's mind, losing seventy pounds is impossible. So he doesn't even try. It simply can't be done.

But what if Joseph set an initial goal of losing five pounds in five weeks, a pound a week, to get down to 285? That is possible, doable. Then 280, 275, and so on. Succeeding by losing five pounds every five weeks could get Joseph down to a healthier, happier weight. After a year, Joseph weighs 238.

He feels better and he looks better. He has stayed with a plan and he might choose to keep going until he weighs 215 or 220.

All this is speculation. Luckily, I can't speak from personal experience. Using this line of reasoning, what am I missing?

One argument I've heard is that empty calories are cheaper than foods with more nutrition. People won't or feel they can't pay more money for more expensive food, even if it is better for them. I suggest that many of these same people waste a lot of their money on fast food, which is usually high in calories, fat, sodium, and cholesterol.

Obesity is on the rise worldwide, but it is almost epidemic in the United States. Obese people live shorter lives than people with healthy weights, and their healthcare costs are higher. Some of the diseases and conditions related to obesity are diabetes, heart disease, back pain, skin infections, infertility, high blood pressure, cancer, and gallstones.

To some extent, obesity, like smoking, is a socioeconomic phenomenon. Better educated folks with more access to information and more awareness of the dangers of poor eating habits are a bit less likely to be overweight.

So if you, dear reader, are overweight, please do something for yourself and the people who love you. Lose a couple of pounds. Repeat as needed. You'll feel better and enjoy a much improved quality of life.

CHAPTER 13

Loose Ends

1. We have a Coinstar machine in our store. People bring in a bag or a bucket of loose change and feed the money into the machine, which counts the money, charges a fee of approx 9 percent of the gross amount, and prints a voucher for the net amount. The customer brings the voucher to a cashier to cash it in or pay for purchases.

Paying 9 percent is a large premium to pay. Most casinos in Reno will count and cash in your change for free.

The lowest net ticket I ever cashed in was $1.23. The customer wanted a dollar bill.

2. One of our associates was allegedly fired for trying to look up the skirts and dresses of our female customers. Allegedly, he would lie on the floor in the register area and pretend to clean around the check stands. The mirror he was allegedly using was to help him see the areas on the floor that needed cleaning.

3. At "my" Walmart, our restroom sinks have cool water, not warm or hot. The sink in the break room has hot water. A semicompulsive hand washer, I use the sink in the break room at every opportunity. Regardless of where you shop, I hope you wash your fruits and vegetables before you eat them.

4. You have to be eighteen or older to buy spray paint and sharpie markers. You have to be sixteen or older to buy a hunting knife.

5. I have to be careful not to roll my eyes, shake my head, drop my jaw, smirk, or laugh out loud at some of the things I see. Moderation is often the best way to go, but I have trouble moderating myself. I am extremely judgmental, and I hate to see people who make freaks out of themselves with excessive tattoos, disfiguring piercings, and stupid hair. They seem to be screaming, "Look at me! Look at me!"

I really have trouble with the half-dollar-sized holes in the earlobes. And I feel sad when I see older people with heavily tattooed arms and skin that is going slack. Especially women.

6. I hate whistling. People who whistle in public places are putting everyone within hearing range at their mercy. It is a selfish and inconsiderate act to whistle in public. Please don't do it. It's more than annoying. It makes me feel angry, and I don't want to feel angry.

7. One night I cashiered for a family of seven—mom, dad, five little kids. They spent $300 on food and paid with WIC and food stamps. Then they bought a DVD for $24.95 plus tax. For some reason, this really bothered me.

8. One way to entertain oneself is to go online and look up peopleofwalmart.com or Walmartians or beartales.me. You'll get access to dozens and dozens of bizarre photos of Walmart shoppers.

9. One evening I walked into the break room and saw seven younger associates (let's say twenty-five and under) seated at the various tables. Six associates were holding their cell phones up to their ears or in front of their eyes. The seventh had his phone on a table, and he was staring at the phone but not touching it.

You have probably heard the expression, "May you live in interesting times." You've also heard the expression "Get a life."

CHAPTER 14

Baseball

In the first chapter, I mentioned that I am a baseball fan. And what would a book about cashiering at Walmart be without a chapter on baseball? So here are a few paragraphs about some things I DON'T like about baseball, but even as I write about them, I acknowledge that they all play a part in making the game what it is. These are not deep thoughts. They are simply a few general observations.

UMPIRES

I am not satisfied with the quality of the umpiring in major league baseball. Admittedly, the personal opinions of an old man who works at Walmart will not have any effect on MLB umpiring, but this old man asserts that the umpires make too many mistakes.

Behind the plate, the umpires have different strike zones, and that is fine as long as the calls are consistent throughout the game. The players, coaches, and managers are entitled to know what to expect. Too often, though, an umpire will expand or contract the strike zone, perhaps around the sixth or seventh inning, and the consistency the players depend on disappears.

And some umpires are inconsistent throughout the game. No need to mention names, but I will mention some anyway. Some of the more controversial umpires are C. B. Bucknor, Joe West, and "Balkin Bob" Davidson. It's interesting to read the MLB players' opinions about the various umpires.

For many years I have felt that the umpires on the bases miss far too many calls. The TV replays, using slow motion, have backed up my opinion; and up until the 2014 season, the umpires have not had the benefit of instant replay.

Sometimes the umps are not in a good position to see the play. Well, part of the job is to get into position, if at all possible, to see the play clearly. As with most endeavors, "perfect practice makes perfect." Supposedly, umpires are trained to concentrate, see, and hear. They can and should do much better.

And maybe they will. It's too soon to draw conclusions about the new replay rules, but these are my first impressions. My take is that the replay rules will improve the accuracy of the final calls in two ways. Obviously, some of the replay rulings will reverse the umpires' original calls. Secondly, (I'm hoping) the umpires will be embarrassed into being better at what they do. If they fear that their original calls will be reversed by the replay officials, they might concentrate more and get a higher percentage of the calls right the first time.

One parting shot on this topic. I'm amazed at the selection of certain umpires to work in the post-season games. The umpires selected to work post-season are supposed to be the best of the bunch and some of them are not.

NOT HUSTLING

Major League Baseball's season covers many months—spring training, a long 162- or even 163-game season, and post-season play. Some players get injured. All players get tired, except for Hunter Pence. It's not easy to be at the top of one's game every minute, but attitude and commitment go a long way.

When Theo and I talk about hustling in baseball, she always mentions Charlie Rose. Theo means Pete Rose, who was often called "Charlie Hustle." Charlie Rose is a well-respected journalist, news anchor, and talk show host. Would you believe that his full name is Charles Peete Rose, Jr.? It really is. Alas, his best sport was basketball, not baseball.

Pete Rose is a very controversial person. Over the years, many thousands of words have been spoken and written about his alleged gambling and his exclusion from the Hall of Fame. Whether you love him or hate him, most fans and pundits agree that Pete Rose hustled.

And he still holds many MLB and national league records.

Back to hustling or not hustling. After hitting a routine grounder or fly ball, some players jog to first base instead of running hard. This lack of effort makes no sense to me. In baseball, bridge, bingo, whatever, always give your opponent the opportunity to make a mistake.

Stretching a single into a double takes speed and recognition. The players who can regularly do this depend more on their vision and reflexes than on their first base coaches. Some players don't run well.

That's okay. But some players don't run. That's not okay.

SPORTSCASTERS' GRAMMAR

I don't expect athletes to use proper grammar all the time even if they happen to be college graduates.

Too many "student-athletes" are really athletes passing through high school and college pretending to be students. I don't like it, but that's just the way it is.

I am dismayed at the number of mistakes the broadcasters make. Some of these folks are very well known, and if I mentioned their names, you might recognize those names. In this case, I won't mention names because some of my favorite broadcasters murder the English language.

When to say "amount" and when to say "number" is one mistake I hear almost every time I watch or listen to a game. Amount of hits, amount of RBIs. Wrong! "Amount" refers to a quantity—the amount of pine tar on a baseball bat or on a pitcher's fingers, the amount of debris littering the outfield on a windy day. "Number" refers to people or items that can be counted—a large number of people in the upper deck, the number of hits and walks that make up a pitcher's WHIP. We could talk about singular mass nouns and plural count nouns, but let's not. I think I've made my point.

Many broadcasters have trouble with their pronouns. They mix up their objective pronouns and their subjective pronouns. "Between you and I" is wrong.

It's "between you and me." One that really annoys me is using "he" instead of "him" as in "Smith was playing in shallow center and the ball went between he and Jones."

There are countless other mistakes that broadcasters make every day, but on this particular topic, we are done.

IN THE NEIGHBORHOOD

One of the most interesting calls made by an umpire is the "in the neighborhood" call at second base. This play typically happens with a runner on first and a ball hit to the second baseman. The second baseman fields the ball and flips it to the shortstop, who is near second base, but he may not actually touch the base, usually because he is trying to avoid being taken out by the base runner coming from first base. So even though the shortstop never touches the base, the umpire calls the runner out. The shortstop then throws the ball to the first baseman to try to complete the double play. There are many variables; for example, the ball is hit to the shortstop who tosses the ball to the second baseman—or the pitcher takes the relay throw at first base.

Much discussion has centered around the "in the neighborhood" play. Some justify the "out" call because of the danger the fielder at second base encounters when the base runner slides with cleats high or when the base runner runs into the fielder. Of course, the runner can also be injured.

Others think the call at second base should be "out" only if the fielder touches second base or tags the runner.

BOOING THE OPPOSITION

When the visiting pitcher throws to first base to attempt a pickoff play or to check a runner, the home team fans always boo. And when the visiting team decides to intentionally walk a batter, the home team fans boo. I understand that many fans enjoy booing. I usually don't like booing. Booing shows disapproval. I can understand showing disapproval for a dirty play or unsportsmanlike behavior. In situations like these, booing might be acceptable. Showing disapproval for a pitcher's throw to first or a manager's decision to issue an intentional walk shows ignorance of the strategy being employed at that specific moment. When the team you are cheering for makes similar plays, do you boo?

I thought not.

On the other hand, literally, I encourage applauding good plays and performances, regardless of which player or team makes the play. And I do this. It sounds silly, and it probably looks ridiculous, but when I'm watching TV and I see an outstanding play, I sit there and clap my hands, even when the play is executed against the team I'm rooting for.

CHAPTER 15

Thinking inside the Box (Store)

After working part-time for three years as a Walmart cashier, I have spent many hours observing the associates I work with. Many of them seem to be nice, polite, and respectful; unfortunately, the characteristic that most of them share, in my opinion, is mediocrity.

Very few are sharp or bright or witty or quick or noticeably intelligent. Very few are educated beyond their having a high school diploma, which doesn't count for much in the USA. So the people who get promoted are not terribly bright. They are, perhaps, the best of the mediocre.

I think this is what Walmart wants. For the most part, Walmart is not able to hang on to really sharp, well-educated folks, who stay with the company and continue to climb higher in terms of position and income. Instead, most of the bright ones take advantage of better opportunities with other companies.

These are broad, general statements, possibly unfair and perhaps inaccurate, but these thoughts really do reflect my thinking.

Walmart seems to be happy with people with average brains who are capable of following Walmart's guidelines, not thinking "outside the box" because that kind of thinking is too hard to control. It leads to innovation and exception. Walmart does not want innovation and exception because their cookie-cutter approach makes a ton of money. It works. I don't know if this is true or not, but I have read that the Walton family is worth more than the poorest one hundred million Americans combined.

I have worked for two store managers (store managers rarely have any contact with cashiers) and neither one impressed me very favorably. That's okay. They didn't think very much of me either.

The four co-managers in our store answer directly to the store manager; although at this instant, we are without a store manager, and we're waiting for a new one. These four seem to be reasonably bright, but the seven assistant managers who answer to them are duds, drones, and/or robots.

Of the seven assistant managers, three were working at the store when I first started. One calls me by my name, but it took over two years for that to happen; one calls me by my name if he sees my name tag; and one, Lana, has never mentioned my name, but sometimes she says "hi." You'll read more about Lana in a few pages. In three years, I have seen fourteen or fifteen assistant managers.

I cannot imagine that our Walmart shoppers actually enjoy the Walmart shopping experience. Dealing with crowded aisles, crying babies, empty shelves, insanity in the parking lots, and indifferent Walmart associates cannot be fun, but the prices are low enough to make all the aggravation of shopping at Walmart tolerable.

I know there are exceptions to my perceptions. Some Walmart associates are brilliant (3 percent) and some Walmart customers (21 percent) truly enjoy shopping at Walmart. You may not agree with my statistics, but you get the point. My guess is that many of the talented, brighter Walmart associates quickly catch on to the system, get frustrated, and move on to better situations in other companies.

Brain drain.

I was brought on board as a part-time associate. And I think that most of our associates are part-time. Part-time folks don't have all the benefits that full-time people have. And theoretically, full-time associates work more hours than part-time associates. I say theoretically because I recently heard Elena, a full-time associate, complain that she was scheduled to work only twenty-two hours in a week.

Many of the part-time associates are given twenty-five to thirty-two hours a week. In this situation, Elena was assertive and she asked the manager who did the scheduling on which scheduled day off did the manager want Elena to work. The manager chose a day, and Elena picked up eight more hours, giving her thirty hours for that week. But thirty is not forty. And ten hours a week are really important to lower-income people. I'm guessing Elena's hourly rate is around $12. She's worked at Walmart for seven or eight years. (Assuming their annual performance reviews are satisfactory, reasonably competent associates at our store earn an increase of $0.40 an hour each year.) Ten hours a week at $12 an hour times fifty-two weeks is $6,240. Over the course of a year, thirty hours a week would pay Elena $18,720 in base pay. Forty hours would pay her $24,960.

But why give Elena forty hours when you can hire new cashiers and pay them $8.65 an hour? Using this strategy, saving two, three, four dollars an hour, and repeating it thousands of times in thousands of stores eventually adds up to billions of dollars, a few quarters at a time.

On October 20, 2013, I submitted a note to the store manager, Carolyn. You may recall from the chapter about the liquor store that there has been a precedent set when I submit anything in writing—it gets ignored. It is not acknowledged. Here is what I submitted.

October 20, 2013

Three Suggestions

1. We know that some people look for receipts in the store or in the parking lot, find items on the shelves that match

the receipts, and "return" these items for credit or refunds.

Increasing awareness among all associates, especially cashiers, will minimize the success of the thieves who do this. We should destroy all receipts not taken by our customers. Shred them, tear them, (the receipts, not the customers), make sure they cannot be used for this purpose.

We could even have a competition with modest awards for associates who turn in the most "stray" receipts.

2. Some cashiers are still putting hangers and plastic bags in the trash. Hangers, plastic, cardboard, hard-board, bottles, and cans should all be recycled. Walmart associates should be good citizens and part of being a good citizen is caring enough about each other to recycle.

3. Even though my last annual review stated that I would be a good candidate for CSM or Dept. Mgr, my third or fourth attempt at being promoted to CSM recently failed. Someone does not want me to be a CSM, and I have withdrawn that preference. I'm not complaining, but I am wondering why.

So here's my suggestion—when an associate is not selected for a promotion, a manager should take five minutes to sit down with the associate to explain, "Here's why you were not selected for this promotion. Here are some ways you can increase your chances of being selected next time."

Intelligent feedback will help us to feel valued and cared about. Obviously, we work for a paycheck, but we also need to know, once in a while, that we are valued and appreciated.

Respectfully submitted,
Ronn Medow
Cashier

I thought these suggestions were valid and useful. Evidently, Carolyn did not agree with me. Once again, I received no response or acknowledgement. I cannot see how or why these ideas would cause a problem or come into conflict with any current or established store policies. Reminds me of that old joke, "What's the difference between ignorance and apathy?" The answer is "I don't know, and I don't care." (Thanks to Mike Freid, who first told me that joke almost forty years ago.)

Speaking of ignorance and apathy, the following incident happened in December 2013. We had snow on the ground and plenty of Christmas shoppers. I was walking into the store to start my shift. An elderly couple stopped me and the woman told me there was snow and ice in the "crip" area, meaning the handicap parking, and it was difficult to get in and out of the car. I was surprised at her use of the word "crip." I would never use a word like that. I kept that thought to myself and assured her that I would talk to a manager immediately. And I did.

I found Assistant Manager Lana and told her about the customer's complaint. Lana shrugged and made a face as if to say, "What do you want me to do about it?" Then she turned away from me to address something important.

In this situation, my priorities were (1) safety of the customers and the Walmart associates and (2) protect the store from a liability claim. Of course, my concerns mean nothing, but Lana should have taken action to address the complaint. This particular incident is much worse than mere mediocrity—it shows incompetence on the part of Lana. And indifference. And dare I say it? Yes, I dare. Stupidity!

Dozens of times I have said out loud or muttered to myself, "If you can't be excellent, at least be competent." Competent would be a big improvement.

But please keep in mind—what do I know? I just talk to the customers!

CHAPTER 16

Statistics

There are statistics scattered throughout this book, and I think it's important to let you know that 79 percent of all statistics are inaccurate, and 31 percent are actually made up. So wherever and whenever you read statistics, you might want to be 97 percent skeptical and 99 percent aware of this information.

That said, in this book, virtually all the statistics, including the ones in the paragraph above, are made up. This is not necessarily a bad thing because you have every right to disagree with my statistics, and you can mentally or even physically cross out my numbers and fill in your own.

Parenthetically, over the years, Theo and I have had countless discussions that ended with one of us saying, "It doesn't matter."

APPENDIX

Originally, I planned to use the appendix as an overflow tank. Optional reading that might contain too much detail would go into the appendix. Then, as I continued writing and continued reading what I wrote, I realized that over half of what I was writing might be too much detail (boring) for many of you readers. I've never seen a book with an appendix longer than the text of the book itself. It could be the start of a new trend. No, I decided. The readers can choose for themselves what to read and what to skip. If you miss something important, it's your loss. Or perhaps it's your gain. It's so subjective, right?

I thought about removing my appendix, so to speak. Admittedly, it takes a lot of gall and intestinal fortitude to stomach all this blah, blah, blah. I'm just trying to deliver a good ex-spleen-ation of why there is an appendix.

Come on. Have a heart.

AFTERWORD

Thank you! I hope you enjoyed reading this little book. Perhaps it was not what you expected. It certainly wasn't what I expected. Too much nonsense. Not enough substance.

But please keep in mind that you probably have read many books. Eighty-three percent of all American adults have not read a book in the past year. Eleven percent have read one or two books in the past year. So six percent of us are doing all of the reading. (Please refer to the previous chapter on statistics and my disclaimer.)

Back to my point, assuming there is one. You've read this book, and it's doubtful that this is the only book you've ever read. Chances are you have read dozens or even hundreds of books.

As a reader, you have experience. As a writer, I'm a rookie. I've written one little book. And I barely got that done.

I put a lot of weird stuff in this book because it might be my only shot. It took seventy-one years for me to write my first book. One book every seventy-one years could imply that two books will take 142 years. Probably not gonna happen.

On the other hand, you might have noticed my reference to "The Walmart Cashier Strikes Again" in chapter 3. This could be the start of "The Cashierhood" series.

Watch out, Fern Michaels. I'm just getting started.

ABOUT THE AUTHOR

Photo By: Rivkah Beth Medow

Ronn Medow appears to be a reasonably nice old man. At the age of 19, Ronn, who was not a reasonably nice young man, told his family and friends that he wanted to be a writer. Over the next fifty-plus years, Ronn did a number of different things and writing was not one of them. Now, all these decades later, he has finally written a remarkably short book, The Walmart Cashier. At least he wrote something.

Ronn is extremely modest and self-deprecating. There are many, many valid reasons for him to be this way. Read this book and you will agree. He has a wide variety of interests, including baseball and other sports, history with emphasis on U.S. Presidents and Vice-Presidents, politics, and reading. Interests are not necessarily passions. Ronn's passions are his children and grandchildren.

Ronn and his little bride, Theo, have been married for 50 years. If you knew Theo, you would be much more impressed with Ronn, possibly even amazed.

CPSIA information can be obtained
at www.ICGtesting.com
Printed in the USA
FSOW02n1127240616
21965FS